Flight

Hilary Devonshire

FRANKLIN WATTS
London/New York/Sydney/Toronto

© Franklin Watts 1992

Franklin Watts
96 Leonard Street
London EC2A 4RH

Franklin Watts
14 Mars Road
Lane Cove
NSW 2066

UK ISBN: 0 7496 0851 X

10 9 8 7 6 5 4 3 2 1

Series Editor: Hazel Poole
Edited by: Cleeve Publishing Services Limited
Design: Edward Kinsey
Artwork: Aziz Khan
Photography: Chris Fairclough
Consultants: Henry Pluckrose, Margaret Whalley

A CIP catalogue record for this book is
available from the British Library

Typeset by Lineage, Watford

Printed in the United Kingdom

CONTENTS

EQUIPMENT AND MATERIALS

This book describes activities which use the following:

Adhesives (PVA, UHU)
Adhesive tape – 12mm wide, clear
       – masking tape
Balloon (long)
Balsa wood (assorted)
Beads
Blu-tack
Brushes – for glue and paints
Bulldog clip
Card – strong
    – thin
Cardboard tubes
Coins
Craft knife
Cutting board
Drinking straws (plastic)
Elastic bands
Fabric (synthetic)
Fabric crayons
Feathers
Football (small)
Hairdryer
Iron
Marbling inks

Matchstick
Modelling clay
Needle (large)
Paints (acrylic)
Pair of compasses
Paper – carbon paper
    – newspaper
    – squared (1cm) paper
    – tissue-paper
    – tracing paper
    – white drawing paper
Paper clips
Pencil
Pens – felt-tip, black
Pins (sewing)
Propeller unit (wing 7.5cm, obtainable from model shops)
Ruler (also, metal safety ruler)
Sandpaper
Scissors
Sticks – garden sticks
    – wooden meat skewers
Table-tennis balls
Thread (strong)
Washers (metal)

INTRODUCTION

Flight has always fascinated mankind. Watching birds flying freely, people would dream of flying themselves. Long ago, people thought that if they made themselves wings they would be able to fly, but of course their bodies and bones were too heavy to be lifted and their arms were too weak.

As the centuries passed, the understanding of flight grew. Through studying flying creatures, kites, hot-air balloons and gliders, knowledge of the mechanics of flying developed. Today, airliners carrying passengers and heavy cargo are able to travel around the world. Concorde can fly even faster than sound – it is the world's only supersonic airliner.

By following the investigations in this book you will learn something about the science of flight. You will explore the forces which act upon objects moving in the air and how craft which are heavier than air are able to fly.

At the start of each section there are some scientific ideas to be explored.

You will be a scientist. A scientist looks at ideas and tries to discover if they are always true, and will also investigate to see if they can be *disproved.* A scientist is curious and wants to find out about the world. A scientist tests ideas, makes investigations and experiments, and tries to explain what has happened. Your results may be surprising or unexpected, and you may find that you will need to make a new investigation or test a new idea.

You will also be an artist and designer. In each section you will be designing models, and through working with the various materials and techniques, you will make discoveries about the forces of flight. It is not always easy to make a successful flying object. It takes care and patience to obtain the correct balance, weight and symmetry, and to overcome gravity and the air's resistance – but it is great fun to try! Your finished artwork, designs and models will be a record of your scientific findings.

GRAVITY – A DOWNWARD PULL

If you drop an object, or throw it up into the air, it will always fall downwards because of an invisible force called gravity. Gravity pulls everything towards the centre of the Earth. If there was no air around us, everything would fall straight to the ground.

Very light objects, such as dandelion seeds, can float on the air. The air supports them, and resists their fall. Heavy objects fall quickly, pushing the air away. If an object has a large surface area, more air is able to push against it and support it. This slows the object's descent.

Stand on a chair and drop a feather and a marble at the same time. Which do you think will reach the ground first? Try this experiment with other objects. You could use two pieces of paper – one crumpled and one flat; a paper clip; a leaf; a coin. Drop them in pairs and compare their falls.

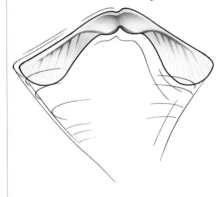

Gravity pulls the seeds down towards the Earth.

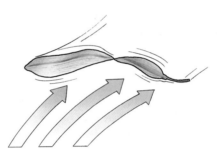

Air pushes against the wings and resists the seed's fall.

The huge expanse of a parachute lets the parachutist fall slowly to the ground and land safely.

Paper wings

You will need: paper, scissors, Blu-tack and felt-tip pens.
1. Cut out an assortment of different paper shapes – a square, a triangle, a circle, a rectangle. Roll a piece of Blu-tack into a ball – this will be a "seed". Attach a seed to each paper shape. Stand on a chair and drop your shapes one by one. Which shaped wing helped your seed to stay in the air the longest? Experiment by putting the seed in different positions on your paper shapes.

2. Can you adapt your shapes to make your seed remain airborne for longer?

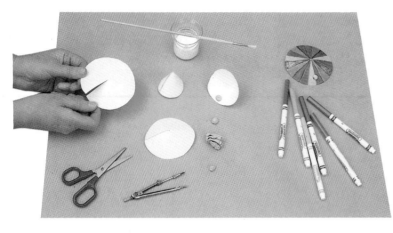

3. A falling winged seed. Does it spin as it falls?

A parachute

You will need: white card, a pair of compasses, a pencil, a ruler, scissors, fabric (synthetic), PVA adhesive, a brush, thread, a needle, paper, fabric crayons and an iron.

1. Cut a circular card template (diameter 10cm). Make eight holes at an equal distance around the circumference of the circle, 1cm in from the edge.

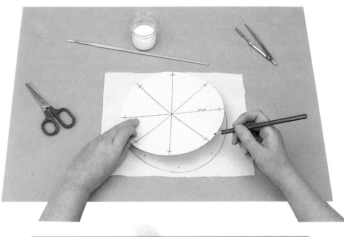

2. Use the template to draw the outline of your parachute on the fabric. With a pencil, mark the eight points and the centre through the holes in the template. Cut out the parachute. Strengthen the edge with a little dilute PVA glue. This will stop it from fraying.

3. Cut eight pieces of thread, 30cm long. Make a double knot at one end, and mark a point 7cm from the other end of each thread. Here the threads have been fixed with masking tape onto a sheet of cellophane to hold them still while marking.

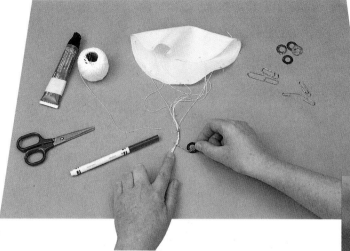

4. Thread the threads through the eight points of the parachute and secure them with a tiny spot of glue. With another thread, tie the threads at the marked points and glue it to prevent the join from slipping. Attach a washer to the end of the parachute.

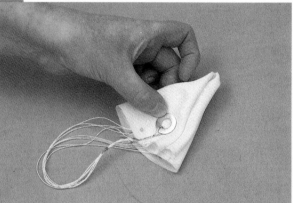

5. Test your parachute in a safe place. Fold the parachute and throw it high into the air. Watch it carefully as it descends.

6. Cut a small hole in the centre of your parachute. This vent will allow the air to escape through the centre so that the parachute can descend more evenly. Outside on a still day, the parachute should fall straight down.

Experiment with different shaped canopies: a square, a rectangle. Try different materials: a kitchen towel, plastic. If you add more washers, what happens? Remember these design factors:
● The vent should be exactly in the centre of the parachute.
● The vent should not be too large, nor the weight of the object too heavy, or the parachute will fall too fast.

A decorated parachute

1. Use the fabric crayons to draw your design onto white paper.

2. Place the design face down on a piece of synthetic fabric and place this between two clean sheets of paper on a thick pad of newspaper.

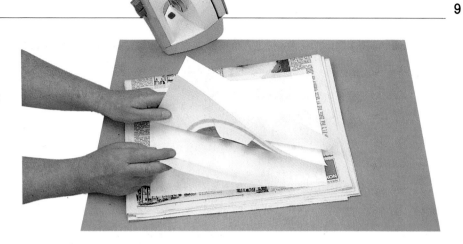

3. With a hot iron, press steadily over the design to transfer the pattern to the fabric.

WARNING: ASK AN ADULT TO HELP YOU WITH THE IRON. YOU COULD EASILY BURN YOURSELF OR THE FABRIC.

4. Two decorated parachutes, ready for testing.

5. A successful fall.

GOING UP

If gravity always pulls objects downwards, why can some animals or objects move upwards through the air? A bird flaps its wings, pushing the air downwards to make it rise. Moving air, a breeze or a stronger wind, can blow objects upwards.

Some gases are lighter than air. A balloon filled with helium will float upwards into the air because the helium is lighter. Warm air is lighter and will rise above colder, heavier air. A hot-air balloon is made to rise by heating the air inside the balloon. It is a lighter-than-air craft.

Watch a bird fly upwards into the sky. Notice how it moves its wings.

Have you flown a kite? Is it easier to lift the kite into the air on a windy day?

Have you seen a hot-air balloon rise into the sky? Read about the Montgolfier brothers from France who designed the first hot-air balloon.

A bird uses its wings to push the air downwards so it can fly.

Moving air, a wind, gives lift to a kite.

Miniature kites

You will need: squared (1cm) paper, a pencil, a ruler, thin card, scissors, a craft knife, metal ruler, tissue-paper, thin balsa wood, glue, paper, a paper clip and some thread.

1. Draw a kite shape (height 19cm, width 16cm) on the squared paper. This is your pattern. Use the pattern to cut a card template, and then use this template to cut your kites from the tissue paper.

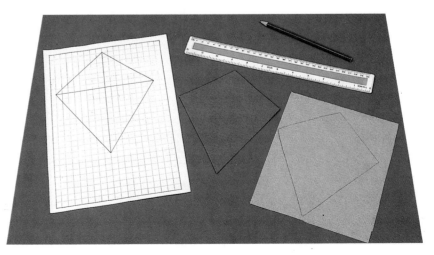

2. Cut two balsa wood strips, 7.5mm wide, for the kite frame. Glue them together at right angles, at the centre. Use a little glue to stick the tissue kite to the frame.

3. Cut some strips of tissue paper for the kite tail. Stick each strip to the previous one at the centre. Attach the tail to the kite.

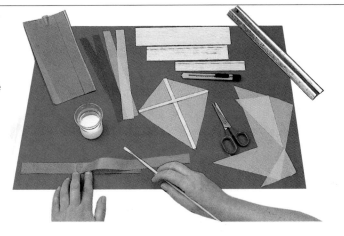

4. Make a 1cm fold along the side of a piece of paper, 5× 10cm. Cut and fold back one-third of the folded edge and stick to the frame as shown.

5. Tie a piece of thread to a paper clip and fasten this to the paper at an angle of 45°. Notice the very long tail of the yellow kite.

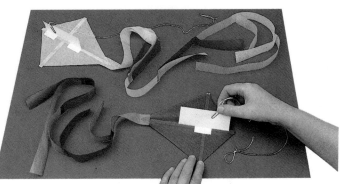

To test the design of your kite, hold the kite by the thread at arm's length. Your arm must be level with your shoulder. Turn around on the spot. If your kite rises above the level of your hand, it has lift. You have made a successful design. You can do this test indoors.

Experiment by putting the paper clip in a different position, or at a different angle. Try to fly your kite with no tail, and then with a very long tail.

6. When you pull on the thread and move with the kite, air pushes against the underside and forces it up into the air.

A hot-air balloon

You will need: a small football, masking tape, a pen, a ruler, scissors, tracing paper, thin card, tissue-paper, dilute PVA adhesive and a hairdryer.

1. Carefully stick masking tape around the ball, dividing it into eight segments. Mark the centre with a pen.

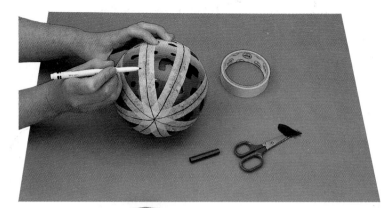

2. Trace the outline of one segment onto tracing paper. Draw a second line 1cm outside the first. Make a card template of this shape and use it to cut out eight tissue-paper segments.

3. Fold the tissue-paper segments in half and make a second fold 5.5cm above the bottom point.

Using the ball as a mould, glue the top half of the tissue-paper segments together in a semi-sphere. Do not glue further than half-way or you will not be able to remove the tissue paper from the ball.

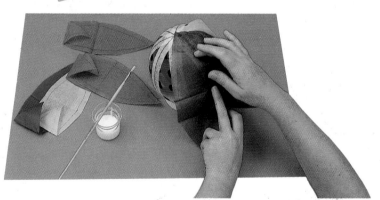

4. Carefully remove the tissue-paper from the ball. Glue the lower half of the segments together, a little at a time, to obtain a rounded shape. Glue as far as the lower fold.

5. Stick a rim of tissue paper around these bottom points and reinforce with a second layer of tissue paper. Leave to dry.

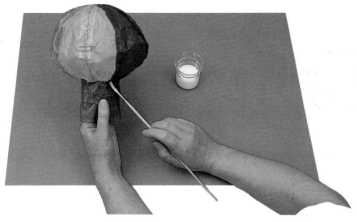

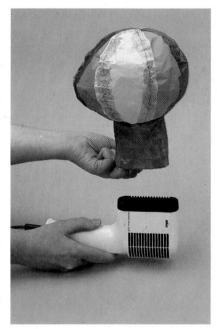

6. Test your balloon. Use a hairdryer to heat the air inside the balloon.

7. You may like to make a basket for the passengers!

SYMMETRY IN FLIGHT

All flying things are symmetrical. They are the same shape on both sides. They need to be symmetrical to balance their weight in flight.

Look at a bird, an aeroplane, and a flying insect. Study their shapes and notice their symmetry. Where is the axis of symmetry?

Read about the flying reptiles which lived on Earth many millions of years ago, but are now extinct.

Flying objects are symmetrical. They are the same shape on either side of their axis of symmetry.

A flying seagull

You will need: paper, a pencil, a sheet of carbon paper, scissors, a matchstick, a craft knife, strong card, glue, paints and a brush, adhesive tape, cotton thread, Blu-tack, coins, metal washers and a wooden bead.

1. Draw the body, one wing and the tail of your seagull on paper, and transfer this to the card using carbon paper. Don't forget to transfer *two* wing shapes. Use a craft knife to cut out the pieces.

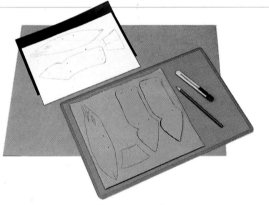

2. Paint the seagull and fit the tail onto the body. Attach the wings to the body with thread and make a hinge underneath with adhesive tape. Add a piece of card on top of the wing near the body to prevent the wings from folding upwards.

3. Thread the cotton through the wings and the piece of card tube so that the seagull hangs straight. Attach the thread to the tube with adhesive tape. Thread a wooden bead on to a length of cotton thread and tie a piece of matchstick to one end. Attach this pull to the body of the seagull.

4. Using Blu-tack, weight the underside of each wing with coins so that the wings are balanced and pull down towards each other.

5. Thread metal washers onto the matchstick on the string pull until the weight is just sufficient to balance the wings outstretched. If the string is lifted, the weight of the wings will pull the wings downwards.

6. Lift and pull the string. The seagull will flap its wings.

FORWARD THRUST

In order for objects to move forward through the air they need a force to propel them. This force is called forward thrust.

We can propel things by hand. In athletics, javelin throwers try to make their javelins travel long distances. The javelins are carefully balanced for weight, and the angle of throw is important.

Early gliders, the first piloted aircraft, were either propelled by a downhill launch, or towed by a rope. They lifted into the air like a kite.

With an adult, study a dart from a darts game. Which is the heaviest part of the dart? Are the fins on different darts all the same shape?
    Read about Sir George Cayley. He was the first man to make a glider by combining the ideas of the thrust of an arrow with the lift of a kite.

We can create forward thrust by hand.

WARNING: ALWAYS HANDLE DARTS WITH CARE; THEY CAN BE DANGEROUS.

Flying sticks

You will need: plastic straws or wooden sticks (with blunt ends) and modelling clay.

Can you make a stick (or straw) travel in the direction you want it to go without it tipping or turning?

Use modelling clay to weight your stick in different positions,

● in the middle
● at the front, then at the back
● at both ends
● in other positions.
    Test your sticks in a safe place. How well do they fly? Which travelled the farthest?
    Try a stick with feathers, or paper fins, at the back.

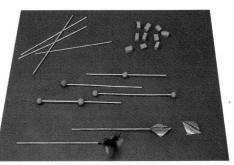

A Cayley glider

In 1804, Sir George Cayley made a glider by fixing a kite shape to a long rod. He made a tail for his glider with two kite shapes set at right angles.

You will need: thin card, a pair of compasses, a pencil, a ruler, scissors, felt-tip pens, a pin, a plastic straw, adhesive tape (12mm wide) and Blu-tack.

1. Draw and cut out the glider as shown. Make two marks on the straw 5cm and 13cm from the tail end. Cut two slits at 90° for the tail fins.

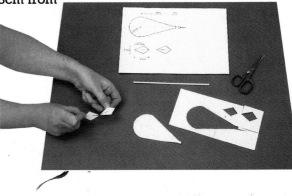

2. Decorate your glider. Join the fins together at right angles and fit them into the tail slits. Use adhesive tape to attach the wing to the straw at the first marked point.

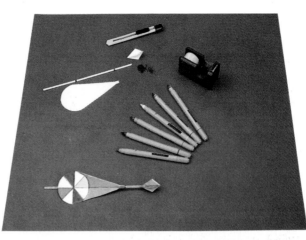

3. Push the pin through the wing, wrap adhesive tape around the pin, and then push the pin through the straw. The tape positions the wing at the correct angle.

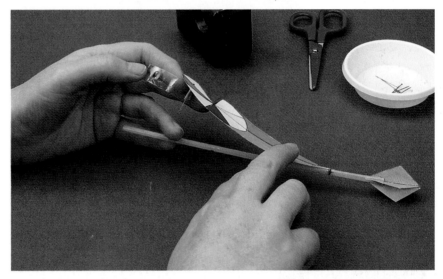

4. Add Blu-tack to the nose of the glider until the model balances at the second point. How well does your glider fly?

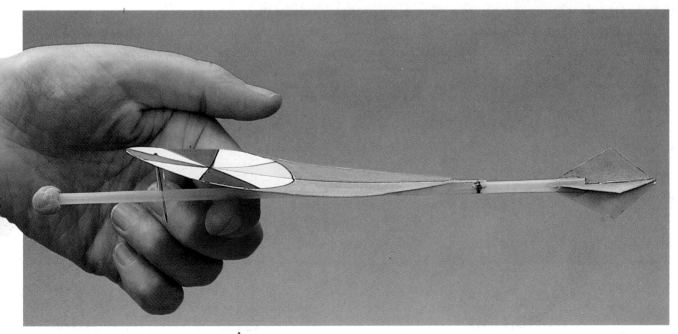

A BACKWARD FORCE

As an object flies through the air, it has to move the air out of the way. The air pushes against the object and slows down its flight. This force of air is called air resistance, or drag, and works in the opposite direction to the forward thrust.

A streamlined object allows the air to pass smoothly over and under it. Aircraft designers try to make their aeroplanes as streamlined as possible to lessen the air resistance.

Study the shapes of the noses of different aircraft. Are they flat, or streamlined? Are they the same shape? Compare early and modern aircraft.

An airship is shaped like a long balloon. It is very streamlined and moves through the air with very little resistance.

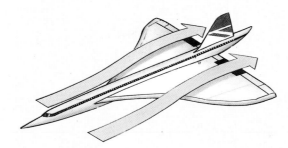

Air can pass smoothly over and under streamlined objects, whether they are natural or man-made.

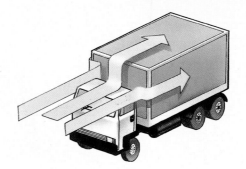

A large, flat, vertical surface creates great air resistance.

A drag test

Try to run holding a large, stiff sheet of card in front of you. Feel the force of the air pushing against the card as you run.

Test fliers

You will need: 2 pieces of card (20×3cm), a sheet of A4 paper, scissors, a pencil, a ruler and Blu-tack.

1. Cut two large and two small pieces of paper from the sheet of A4 as shown. Fold each piece of paper in half, and use the ruler to help you fold back a 2cm strip along the longer side.

2. Attach the folded papers to the pieces of card with Blu-tack. The wings of one flier are folded forward; the wings of the second flier are folded back.

3. Balance the weight of your fliers by adding a small piece of Blu-tack to the body. This prevents the heavier nose from tipping forward.

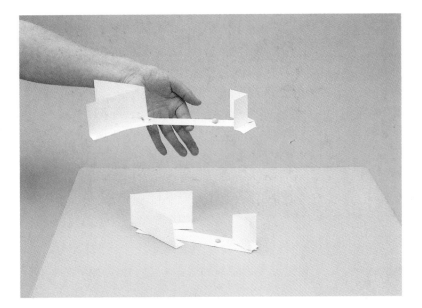

4. Test your fliers. How far do they fly? Which do you think would be the most successful design?

Experiment by folding the wings at different angles, and see which flier travels the farthest.

A balsa wood plane

You will need: squared (1cm) paper, thin balsa wood, a pencil, carbon paper, a craft knife, a metal ruler, masking tape and Blu-tack.

1. Draw your design on squared paper and use carbon paper to transfer it onto the sheet of balsa wood.

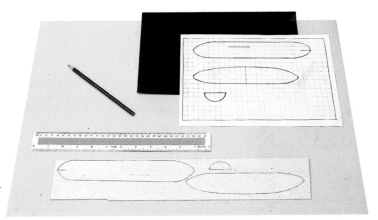

2. Cut out your plane using the craft knife and safety ruler. Carefully cut narrow slits in the body so that the wing and tail fit securely. These can be held in position with masking tape. The shape of the plane should be symmetrical.

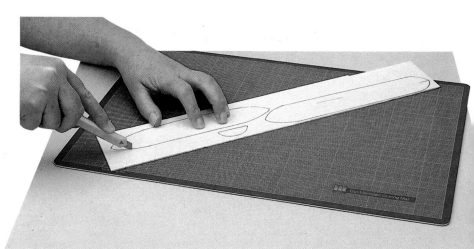

3. If the plane tips upwards in flight, add a little Blu-tack to the nose.

4. Study the plane from the front. There is very little surface to resist the air. It is very streamlined.

You could make another plane with a different wing design and wing position.

AEROFOILS AND FLIGHT

If you study an aeroplane's wing, you will notice that the top surface curves upwards. When the plane is flying, the air moving over the top of the wing has to move faster than the air moving underneath. The wing's special shape is called an aerofoil.

The faster-moving air above the wing spreads out and so has a lower pressure than the slower air underneath. Beneath the wing the higher pressure of air pushes upwards and lifts the plane. If the plane is moving fast enough, this upward pressure has the strength both to lift and support the aircraft in the air.

Look carefully at an aeroplane's wings. Do the tail wings have the same aerofoil shape?

A bird's wing has an aerofoil shape, too. Insect wings, which are much thinner, become more curved in flight.

How many flying animals can you think of? Do they all have wings?

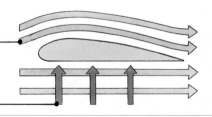

faster-moving air has less pressure

slower-moving air — higher pressure gives lift

Testing the pressure of moving air

You will need: two table-tennis balls, marbling paints, thin sticks, modelling clay, two elastic bands, paper, card, plastic drinking straws, scissors, thread, beads, adhesive tape and a hair dryer.

Table-tennis balls

1. Decorate two table-tennis balls with marbling paints. Leave to dry.

2. Stand two sticks in modelling clay on a piece of card, and secure the horizontal stick with elastic bands. Using thread and adhesive tape, suspend the table-tennis balls at the same height.

Use a straw to blow between the balls. Can you blow them away from each other? Because the moving air between the balls has a lower pressure than the still air on the outside, the balls are pushed together!

Paper flags

1. Make two flags with paper and plastic drinking straws. Stand two sticks, a small distance apart, in modelling clay on a piece of card. Place a bead on each stick.

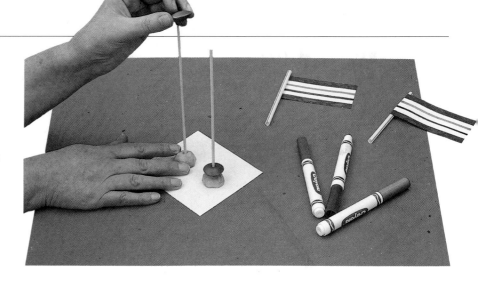

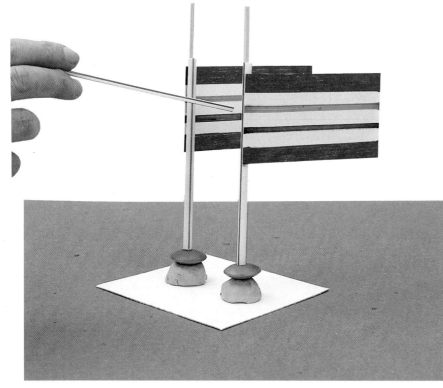

2. Put the flags on the stick supports so that the flags face in the same direction.

Use a straw to blow between the flags. What do you think will happen? Ask your friends to blow them apart!

Paper aerofoils

1. Cut a strip of paper, 20×6cm. Fold it almost in half, leaving a 1cm strip at the end. Pull the top edge across. Join the two edges with adhesive tape. You have made an aerofoil shape which is like an aeroplane's wing.

2. Make two holes and push a straw through the centre, as shown. Secure with a little glue.

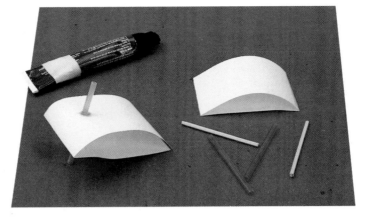

3. Make a stick support as before. Put a small piece of straw on the support, then your aerofoil.

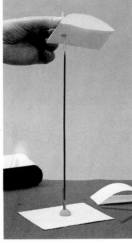

4. Use a hairdryer to blow over and under the aerofoil. It will rise in the air because the air moving across the curved top surface is faster and has less pressure. Your wing has lift-off!

5. Glue together about 1cm at the back of your aerofoil wing. Make two cuts on either side and turn down the edges. This will help to direct the air flow. You could try folding the back flaps up.

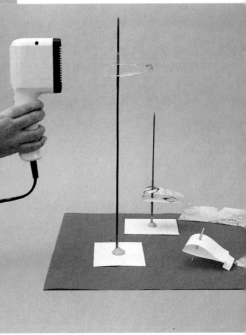

DIRECTION IN FLIGHT

Moving flaps on the wings and tails of aircraft have been designed to control the direction of flight. Air presses against the flaps as they are lowered and raised.

Moving the wing flaps, which are called ailerons, makes a plane tilt and roll. Moving the tail flaps, which are called elevators, makes the plane climb and dive. A tail rudder is used with the ailerons to make the plane turn left and right.

Read about the Wright brothers. Their plane "Flyer" made the first controlled flight. In early aircraft, the pilot had to control the wing and tail flaps with cables.

Find out about the Kramer prize – an early competition to build a man-powered aeroplane that was good enough to fly a figure-of-eight course.

Raising the aileron increases the drag.

Lowering the aileron gives more lift.

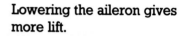

Paper planes

You will need: A4 paper, scissors, a pencil, a ruler and felt-tip pens.

1. Fold a sheet of paper exactly in half in both directions. Fold over 1cm along a long edge. Continue to fold the paper until you reach the centre line. Press hard to make the fold flat.

2. Fold the two wings together and cut out the plane's shape. Open it out flat. The plane is symmetrical. Fold up 1cm for the wing tips and 1cm down for the tail.

3. Camber the back of the wing down between your fingernail and thumb. This makes an aerofoil shape.

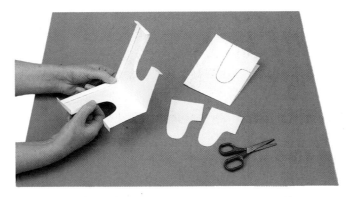

4. Launch your plane by pushing it gently away from you.

Control of your plane

1. If your plane dives, fold it in half and cut two matching tail elevators. Bend them upwards.

2. Cut an aileron in the back of each wing. To make your plane turn left, bend up the left aileron, and bend down the right. To make your plane turn right, bend down the left aileron, and bend up the right. You can decorate your plane with felt-tip pens.

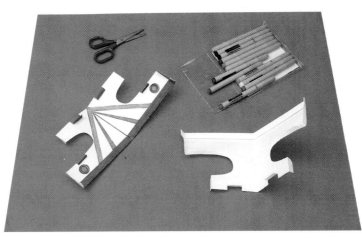

3. There are many different paper plane designs. Remember, a successful flier has to be symmetrical.

You could design a course for paper aeroplanes which will challenge you and your friends in creative aircraft design.

PROPELLED FLIGHT

If gravity pulls everything downwards towards the Earth, how can heavier-than-air craft stay in the air?

To overcome gravity and the air's resistance, a plane needs to have a very powerful forward thrust. The forward thrust of some aeroplanes comes from one or more spinning propellers which are driven by the plane's engines. The propeller blades are twisted. They screw into the air as they turn, pushing the air backwards and the plane forwards.

Jet planes move forward by jet propulsion. The engines force jets of gas out at the back at great speed. These drive the plane forward.

The strong forward thrust of an aircraft, provided by its engines, forces air over and under the aerofoil-shaped wings. This gives the plane lift and supports it during its flight.

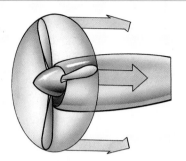

Propeller blades push the air backwards so the plane can move forward.

Study the designs of modern aircraft. Many smaller planes are still driven by propellers, just like the first aeroplanes. Jet planes are expensive and use a lot of fuel, but they can travel at very high speeds.

Find out about the early aviators. Who were the first people to fly? Why is Amy Johnson famous?

A balloon jet flier

You will need: thin card, scissors, a straw, glue, a needle and thread, a long balloon, a bulldog clip and masking tape.

1. Cut a symmetrical wing shape of your own design. Glue a straw to the underside at the centre line. Use a needle to pass a length of thread through the straw.

2. Blow up the balloon and close the end with a bulldog clip. Attach the balloon to the wing with masking tape. The balloon will be the flier's engine.

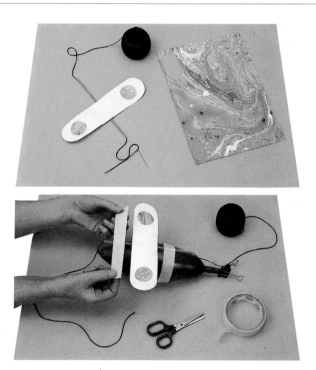

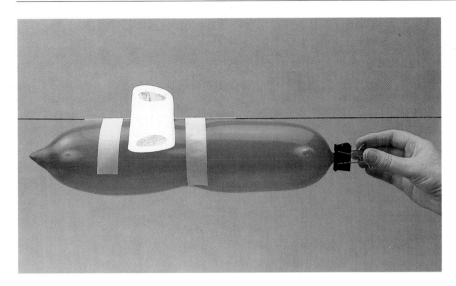

3. Tie the thread tightly in a horizontal position and pull the balloon to one end of the thread. Release the clip and watch the forward thrust of the flier. As the air rushes out, it propels the flier forward – just like a jet engine.

A propeller plane

You will need: balsa wood, squared paper, carbon paper, a pencil, a ruler, a craft knife and safety ruler, a large needle, a paper clip, glue, sandpaper, a 7.5cm propeller unit and a 17cm rubber band.

1. Using the plan, draw the wing and tail of the plane on a piece of thin balsa wood. Carefully cut out the pieces with a craft knife. Remember, balsa wood is very fragile. Cut out the body (27×1.25cm) from a piece of 5mm-thick balsa wood.

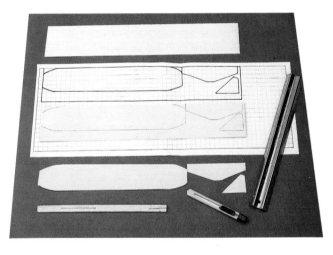

2. Cut a slot, 7cm long, in the body, just wide enough for the wing to pass through. Cut a 3.5cm notch in the back of the body for the tail.

3. Gently sandpaper the edges of the aeroplane parts. Carefully glue the tail pieces into position and gently slide in the wing.

4. Make a hole in the body with the needle, and push in both ends of the piece of paper clip, as shown. Turn up the long end into a hook.

5. Carefully sandpaper the nose of the plane to allow the propeller unit to fit on tightly. Attach the rubber band to act as the motor to drive the propeller. Join the band to the hook in the body.

6. Wind the propeller until the band tightens, and hand launch the model as shown.

Flying tips
● If the plane dives, move the wings forward in the slot.
● If the plane climbs and stalls, move the wings backward in the slot.
● You can correct right or left dives by moving the wing slightly to the right or left. Experiment with the wing's position.

7. You can decorate your plane with felt-tip pens. A thin line of PVA adhesive along the edges which are likely to be damaged on landing will strengthen your plane.

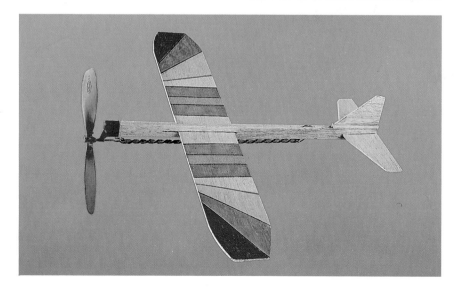

8. Watch your plane fly.

THE FORCES OF FLIGHT

In this book we have looked at the four main forces of flight: the downward pull of weight and gravity, the upward lift, the backward pull of the air's resistance, and the forward thrust. Many inventors and engineers have contributed over the centuries towards the development of today's airliners.

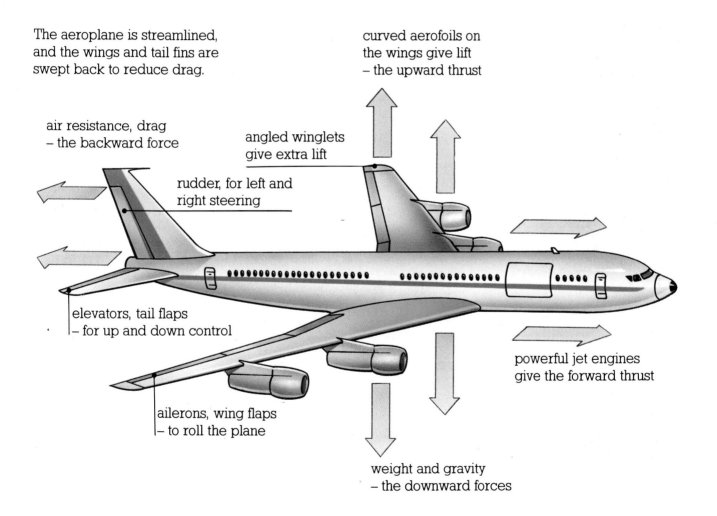

The aeroplane is streamlined, and the wings and tail fins are swept back to reduce drag.

curved aerofoils on the wings give lift – the upward thrust

air resistance, drag – the backward force

angled winglets give extra lift

rudder, for left and right steering

elevators, tail flaps – for up and down control

ailerons, wing flaps – to roll the plane

powerful jet engines give the forward thrust

weight and gravity – the downward forces

FURTHER IDEAS

A paint and crayon picture

1. Make some sketches of the shapes of different aircraft. Cover a piece of thin card with a pattern using light-coloured crayons.

2. Mix some black powder paint and detergent to a creamy consistency and brush this over the crayon pattern.

3. Choose one of your sketches and cut its outline in the wet paint. The colours of the crayon will show through.

4. "Early aircraft".

"Hot-air balloon"

Cut a design in thin card of a flying craft. Glue your design onto a background card. Place a sheet of paper over your design and use wax crayons to make a rubbing.

An illustrated dictionary

Make an illustrated dictionary of words which have links with air and flying.

Here are some examples:

airliner	flying buttress
airport	flying fish
airstrip	flying saucer

A photographic study

Use a camera to take photographs of flight in our world. You may decide to study a variety of airborne objects, and work out what is holding them up in the air.

GLOSSARY

Aerofoil
The name given to the curved surfaces of an aircraft which produce lift.

Aeronautics
The science of flight.

Aileron
The hinged flap on an aircraft wing which alters the lift on either side of the aircraft, causing tilting and rolling.

Aircraft
Any kind of flying machine. Hot-air balloons and airships are lighter-than-air craft. Gliders and powered aeroplanes are heavier-than-air craft.

Air pressure
The effect of the weight of air pressing on an object or substance. Moving air is less dense and so its pressure is lower.

Air resistance
The force of air pushing against an object as it is flying, which slows it down.

Camber
To slightly curve or arch.

Density
The weight of a substance per unit of volume.

Drag
A backward force, caused by air resistance in flight.

Elevator
The tail flap of an aircraft used for climbing and diving.

Flight
Movement through the air with the use of wings.

Force
A pull or push which can cause the movement of an object in direction or speed.

Forward thrust
A force which propels an object forward.

Glider
A light, engineless aircraft which is airborne on moving currents of air.

Gravity
An invisible force which pulls everything down towards the centre of the Earth.

Jet engine
An engine which provides the thrusting power of an aircraft by ejecting gases backward which propel the aircraft forward. The forward thrust is greater at higher altitudes where the air is thinner and the drag is reduced.

Lift
To give an upward direction to something. The force which pushes an aircraft upwards.

Parachute
A fabric canopy which increases air resistance by trapping air. They are used to slow the fall of parachutists or brake the speed of fast-moving planes or vehicles.

Propeller
A set of revolving, twisted blades which screw into the air, pushing the air backwards thus thrusting the plane forward.

Streamlined
Having a slim or smooth and rounded shape which lessens air and water resistance.

Symmetry
The identical size and position of opposite parts, on either side of an axis.

Additional photographs: Zefa 2/3,5.